Siem R

20 Must See Att

By Anton Swanepoel

SIEM REAP

20 Must See Attractions

CAMBODIA TRAVEL GUIDE BOOK

Anton Swanepoel

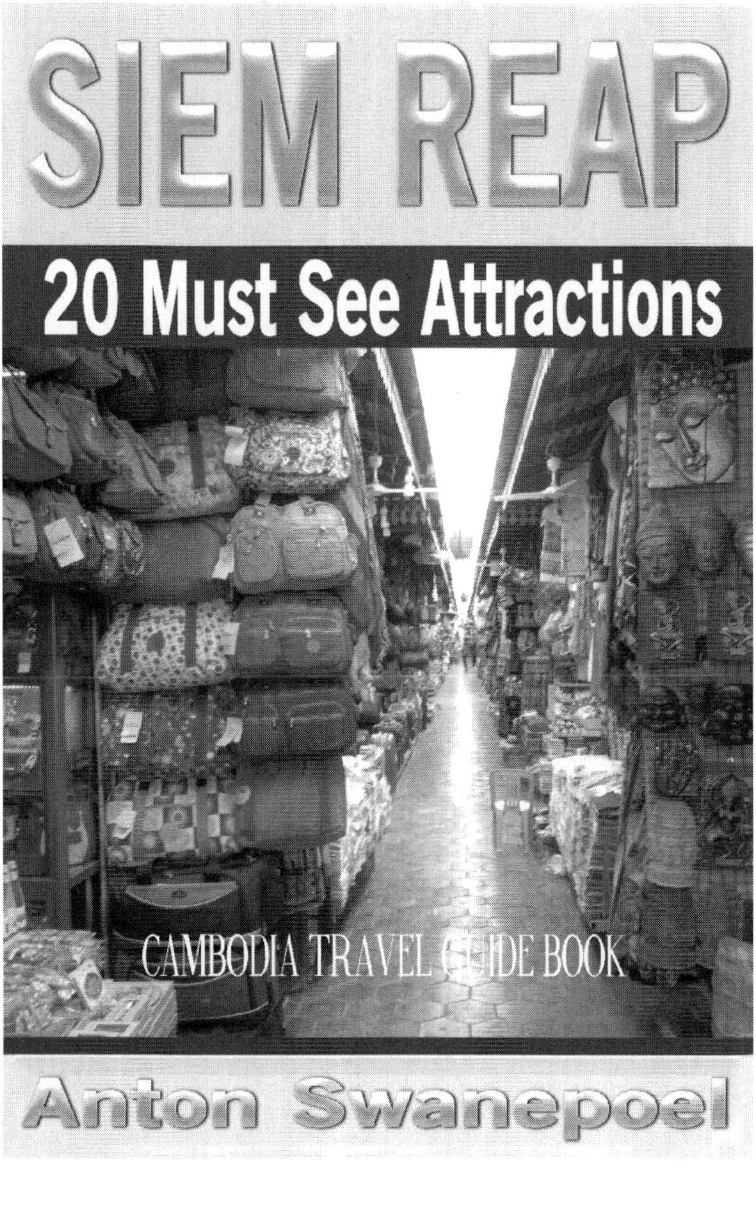

Anton Swanepoel

http://antonswanepoelbooks.com/
http://antonswanepoelbooks.com/blog/
http://www.facebook.com/AuthorAntonSwanepoel
https://twitter.com/Author_Anton

Follow this link if you want updates on new book releases by the Author. http://antonswanepoelbooks.com/subscribe.php
For travel tips follow his blog.

Introduction

Magical Angkor Wat Temple amazes more than two million visitors each year. However, there are a number of things to see in Siem Reap other than temples and pagodas.

This book gives 20 must-see or do attraction, including an additional nine things to do and see. Although some of the items are in the Angkor Wat Park, they are not temples or pagodas.

As these items are additional things to do and see in Siem Reap other than the temples, there is no itinerary for them. Scan though the book and see what attractions you would like to see or activities you would like to do and try to fit them in between temple visits. After reading this book, you may realize that Siem Reap warrants a day or two extra vacation time.

For visitors who are tight on time, this book goes hand in hand with my book **Angkor Wat: 20 Must-See Temples**, which gives you the top 20 temples to see.

If your vacation includes more towns in Cambodia, or Vietnam, Thailand, or Laos, see my books about these places to enhance your holiday.

Note that any company or services I recommend in this book are from my own experience or opinion to use. I have no affiliation with any company nor do I get any returns if you use them. Although I do recommend companies that I have used or found to have a good reputation, life is life, thus I can accept no responsibility for their service.

Table of Contents

Angkor Balloon View

Anton Swanepoel

Time: Around 20 minutes for stationary balloon and 40 minutes a ride for the free-flight balloon.

Importance: Get an overview of Angkor Wat and nearby temples or Siem Reap. See the sunrise and sunset over Siem Reap and Angkor Wat in a different way.

My Impression: Although not cheap, it is still cheaper than going on a helicopter ride. The stationary balloon gives the best value for money, but the free balloon gives the best experience if you can afford it.

Open: 9 am to 5 pm for stationary balloon. Free flight balloon is either sunrise or sunset. Around 6 am for morning flights, and around 5 pm for evening flights. (Times are adjusted to correlate with sunrise and sunset.)

Cost: Adult $15, Children under 12 years old $7.50, for stationary balloon rides. $170 a person for free flight balloon ride. (Promotions go as low as $120 a person at times.)

Entry fee: No Angkor pass needed.

Best time to visit: Sunrise is in my opinion the best for the free flight balloon. For the stationary balloon anytime during the day is okay.

Balloon flights: Angkor Hot Air Balloon.

Website: http://www.angkorballooning.com/

Tel: 855 - 69 558 888 | | **Fax:** 855 - 63 765 788

Email: info@angkorballooning.com

Address: Sivutha Road, Alley old market area.

GPS: 13°24'45.7"N 103°50'59.1"E. For fixed balloon.

Angkor Wat is an important attraction for many visitors to Cambodia. With a balloon ride, you can see this magnificent and famous temple in a new way.

There are two options for balloon rides in Siem Reap. If you are short on time and money or afraid of heights, the stationary balloon is for you. The balloon is one kilometer from Angkor Wat Temple, just outside the security entry and directly opposite the entrance for Angkor Wat Temple.

You do not need an Angkor pass to see the famous temple from the balloon. The balloon is fixed on the spot with a steel cable and allowed to rise between 100 and 200 meters (330 to 660 feet) into the air depending on the weather conditions. At its max height, the balloon offers around 20 kilometers of visibility with a good view of the surrounding area.

To get to the stationary balloon from Angkor Wat, follow the road that starts at Angkor Wat Temple and leads away from the temple. If you want to get to the balloon without entering the Angkor Wat Park, then you have to use the road going past the airport itself and follow it all the way to just before Angkor Wat. The balloon rides are on your left.

Angkor Hot Air Balloon is currently the only balloon flight operator in Siem Reap that offers balloon flights. Each year, they operate only from 1 December to 15 March of the next year. (Dates may be adjusted by the company in advance according to the climate of the current season.) Check their website or contact them for a current schedule before you go if you intend on using them.

The company does two rides a day: a sunrise and a sunset ride. The ride lasts around 40 minutes and offers a view of Siem Reap and Angkor Wat. Takeoff times are 6:10 am to 6:40 am (depending on the season) and 5:00 pm to 5:30 pm (depending on the season). They offer pickup and drop-off service to your hotel. At $170 per person, it is expensive; however, it is a ride of your life.

Know that flights are dependent on weather and may be canceled if the weather does not permit safe flights. You can get a full refund or reschedule for a different day.

Angkor Miniatures

Time: 10 minutes.

Importance: Miniatures of Angkor Wat Temple, Preah Vihear Temple, and a few others.

My Impression: The displays have seen some time in the outdoors, but still give a good impression of the outlay of the temples on show. There are also plans for the outlays of a number of other temples. As the display is right opposite Pre Kor Temple, you can quickly walk across the road and have a look at the miniatures on display.

Open: 6 am to 6 pm.

Entry Fee: None.

Best time to visit: When visiting Pre Kor temple.

GPS: 13°20'52.8"N 103°58'26.4"E for road to turn off from N6.

GPS: 13°20'38.0"N 103°58'26.1"E.

Angkor Miniatures is opposite of Pre Kor Temple and contain miniature displays of Angkor Wat Temple, Preah Vihear, Banteay Srei, Bayon, and Lolei. When visiting Pre Kor Temple, take a quick walk across the road and see how Preah Vihear Temple would look if it was completely restored.

Art for Sale

Time: 10 to 45 minutes.

Importance: Take a memory of Cambodia with you home to show to your friends and family.

My Impression: Cambodian artists are highly skilled, and some of the scenery painted is breathtaking. You can have a portrait painted of yourself at some of the places.

Open: Inside Angkor, the painters are normally there from 9 am to 4 pm. The shops in the new market are normally open from 9 am until late, especially on weekends. The galleries just before Angkor Wat Temple are normally open from around 6 am until 5 pm.

Best time to visit: During the day.

Price: From $10 to $$$$.

GPS: 13°23'14.2"N 103°51'40.3"E. For the shops before Angkor Wat Temple.

Cambodians are very good artists. The details on the temples are just one example. All over Siem Reap, you can buy paintings of different temples in and around Angkor. Some artists will also paint personal portraits for you.

There are a few good places to buy paintings. You can buy some on the scenic road just before you get to the Angkor checkpoint (not the road where you get your entry pass). There are a few galleries displaying art, and most can ship large paintings oversees. Smaller paintings can be taken home inside a hard paper tube.

Another good place is at the new market across the river in town. See New Market/Phsar Kandal for directions. The shops are in the back of the market, near the massage places.

Another place is in the Angkor Wat National Park itself. Here, you will often find artists painting new paintings just outside a temple. Most will paint a painting of you or a specific temple if you ask them. Prices are normally a bit more inside the park, but you can film your masterpiece being painted and have a picture taken with the artist, and that is priceless.

Another good spot is at the New Market, across the road from the central market in town. The shops selling paintings are at the back of the market, near the massage places. See details about the New Market later in the book.

Get a receipt for the painting if you can, as they are cheap, and your country's customs may not believe you bought it for about $20.

Boat Ride

Time: Around 2 hours.
Importance: Tour the Angkor moat and visit Prasat Bei temple.
My Impression: This was one of the nicest boat rides I have had in Cambodia. The only other boat ride that came close was a canoe ride in the mangroves on Tonle Sap Lake.
Open: Around 8 am to 4 pm.
Best time to visit: In the wet season if you can.
Price: $15 for adults and $7 for children.
Website: http://www.kongkearangkor.com/
GPS: 13°25'34.9"N 103°51'22.5"E for boat pick up.

The Angkor Thom City moat ride starts at the south gate and goes up to Prasat Chrung Temple. The ticket office for the rides is close to the south gate bridge. Look for a small freestanding building. Once you get your ticket, follow the dirt road past the ticket office and along the river until you pass a small temple complex (Prasat Bei).

You will see a parking area with the boats by the water. Most operators give you a small bottle of water; however, on hot days, take an extra bottle with you.

The boats normally dock at a small dock at the turnaround point, where you can follow a stairway to see Prasat Chrung Temple. After having seen the temple, the boat will take you back to the starting point. If you want a longer ride, arrange with the ticket office for a personal ride.

You can also do personal canoe rides in the mangroves at Tonle Sap Lake, which is run by the local villages. See Chong Khneas Village under the Tonle Sap Lake attraction for more details.

Banteay Srey Butterfly Centre

Time: 45 minutes.

Importance: Main butterfly farm in Cambodia. See the life cycle of a butterfly and learn more about this magnificent insect. Order pupae and have them shipped to your home if you are a butterfly collector.

My Impression: Learning about the life cycle of butterflies while seeing the different stages was a treat for me. If you are in the area, the butterfly centre is worth a visit.

Open: 9 am to 5 pm, everyday.

Entrance Fee: $4 for adults and $2 for kids.

Website: http://www.angkorbutterfly.com/bbchome.html

Facebook: https://www.facebook.com/pages/Banteay-Srey-Butterfly-Centre/107592649313400

Email: mail@angkorbutterfly.com

Address: Sanday Village, Siem Reap, Cambodia

Telephone: (+855) 0978 527 852

Best time to visit: On your way to the Landmine Museum or Banteay Srey Temple.

Banteay Srey Butterfly Centre is on the same road as Banteay Srey Temple and the Landmine Museum. The center is about three kilometers from the Landmine Museum and around 25 kilometers from Siem Reap. The center is a popular tourist spot and boasts the largest butterfly exhibition in Southeast Asia.

The butterfly center hosts a number of rare and exotic butterflies as well as a number of common ones. The center provides income opportunities for local communities by training farmers to rear butterflies and then helps them sell the butterfly pupae to customers worldwide.

The center allows one to see the full cycle of a butterfly and is a wondrous experience and break from climbing up and down temples. Butterflies are placed in a cage with food plants for the specific butterfly being farmed. Farmers harvest any eggs that were laid by the butterflies and keep them protected. The eggs hatch in around 10 to 14 days. Farmers will then transfer the caterpillar/larvae after hatching onto plants appropriate for the type of butterfly. After around two weeks, the larvae will pupate. When the larvae pupate, they are harvested by the farmers. A portion is held by the farmer for the following breeding cycle, while the rest are sold. Pupae sell for around 50 cents to $2.

The center has a large netted enclosure where a variety of butterflies is free-flying, allowing tourists to marvel at their splendor up close. Some of the butterflies that can be seen are: Atlas Moth, Blue Glassy Tiger, Dark Blue Tiger, Five-Barred Swordtail, Great Mormon, Gaudy Baron, Lime Butterfly, Orange Emigrant, Peacock Pansy, Red Helen, and Tailed Jay. You may also be lucky enough to see a caterpillar morphing into a chrysalis (pupae) or a butterfly emerging from its cocoon.

Bicycle Tours

Time: 1 to 3 hours or more.

Importance: See the countryside, out of the way temples or rural Cambodia villages and rice fields on a bicycle tour.

My Impression: I lived for 1 ½ years in Cambodia, and did many trips though the countryside and local villages. If you have the time to take a break from Angkor Wat, you have to visit some of the local villages and rice fields to experience Cambodian culture. You can rent a bicycle and do it on your own, or go with a tour where you may even eat with locals at their houses.

Open: Depends on the tour operator, however, normally from 8am until the tour is done.

Best time to visit: Dry season for easy riding, rainy season to see wet rice fields. Anytime if only visiting local villages.

Siem Reap may be filled with boutiques, markets, stalls, and small shops; however, the city is surrounded by splendid countryside with rice fields as well as rural villages.

You can also do a bicycle tour to some of the remote temples, such as Banteay Chhmar, or to Kulen Mountain Waterfall.

If you are staying more than a few days in Siem Reap, you can rent a bicycle and then explore the countryside by yourself. Around the Ruolos group temples, a short distance out of town, are nice areas to explore as well as some of the outer temples in the Angkor Wat National Park, such as Prasat Prei and Banteay Prei Temple near Neak Pean Temple or Mangalartha Temple. Going along the Angkor Thom wall to Prasat Chrung Temple is also worth it, so is the path to West Prasat Top and the East and West gate. See Angkor Wat Archeological Park for hidden and out-of-the-way temples.

If you want to go with a bicycle tour company, one to consider is *Grasshopper Adventures.*
Tel: +855 12 462 165.
Website: http://www.grasshopperadventures.com/

If you want to see the temples or the rice fields on your own and find a bicycle to be too much work, you can rent an electric bicycle. See *Green e-bike.*
Email: green_e-bike@outlook.com
Tel: +855 (0)95 700 130/140.
They are open from 7:30 am to 7:00 pm, and have a number of free charge points around town.

If you would rather do a countryside tour on a Vespa, contact *Cambodia Vespa Adventures*:
Tel: +855(0)12 861610 or +855(0)12 861620
Email: info@cambodiavespaadventures.com.
Website: http://www.cambodiavespaadventures.com/

Central Market/Phsar Chaa/Old Market

Time: 1 hour.
Importance: Main market in town, have a number or Khmer restaurants in the market as well as being close to Pub Street.
My Impression: This market is a bit more expensive than the old market on Road 6, as it has become more orientated towards tourists. However, you can still find good bargains at the market, and it is cheaper than the full out tourist market that is a short distance away and across the river.
Open: 7 am to 5 pm.
Best time to visit: Early in the morning to avoid the crowds.
GPS: 13°21'16.2100" N 103°51'19.8200" E.

This market is one of the most visited by tourists in Siem Reap. It stretches a few streets and runs all the way from the river to almost Sivatha (Sivatuh) Boulevard. You can get anything from bedding, pots, and pans to fruit and meat at the market. Clothes and jewelry are also sold at shops in the market.

Note that the market is more based towards tourists and is a bit more expensive than the old market on Route 6, thus do negotiate with prices to a fair degree. Note, however, that the hygiene of the meat is questionable at times, so be careful when buying chicken and fish later in the day. It is best to buy early in the morning to get fresh meat.

There are ATMs across the road at some points if you need to withdraw cash. No shops accept credit or debit cards currently (though this can change). The market is one of your best bets to get cheap clothing, although if you are looking for more upscale stuff, try some of the clothing shops around town.

There are a number of restaurants located on the edges of the market. If you want a bit more upscale restaurants, try Pub Street, which is close by.

Central Park

Time: 45 minutes.
Importance: Main park in Siem Reap.
My Impression: The park is not large compared to other city parks around the world, however, it still gives the opportunity to relax with a good book or a slow walk. The main road is a short distance away, yet it is reasonably quiet in the park.
Open: 24 hours.
Best time to visit: During the day.
GPS: 13°21'47.1600" N 103°51'31.9600" E.

Siem Reap Central Park is a one-city-block park near the Siem Reap River alongside Charles De Gualle Street that leads to Angkor Wat Temple. The park is near a few Khmer restaurants and opposite the Royal Palace in Siem Reap. There are a few benches to sit and relax and well-maintained footpaths that allow for a walk or a jog. The area alongside the river on Charles De Gualle Street from the roundabout near the park, going towards the Central Market, is also worth a walk and has a number of benches to relax on.

Elephant Rides

Time: Around 30 minutes.

Importance: Riding an elephant past ancient temples or up to Phnom Bakheng temple.

My Impression: I took an elephant ride from just outside the South Gate, to Bayon Temple, and fully recommend it. The elephants were well cared for, and the walk was all the way in the shade except for going over the South Bridge. It is something to experience looking down on people sitting in a tour bus.

Open: From 7:30am ~ 10am, or just before sunset at Phnom Bakheng temple.

Best time to visit: The ride up to Phnom Bakheng temple can be booked full, thus an early ride from the South Gate may be a better bet.

GPS: 13°25′33.6900″ N 103°51′34.7100″ E for the pickup at the South Gate.

Currently, you can ride an elephant on two different routes, inside the Angkor National Park.

In the morning from 7:30 am to 10:00 am, you can ride from the south gate in the shade next to the road all the way to Bayon Temple or back. The price is $15, and the ride lasts around 30 minutes.

In the afternoon, from around 4:00 pm, you can ride from the bottom of Phnom Bakheng Temple to the top for $20. The ride takes about 15 minutes. A ride from the top down is $15.

Tips to the mahout are as you wish; he has a tip pocket on the back of his shirt. Tips to the elephants are a bunch of bananas that you can buy from vendors close to the drop-off location.

Note that there are no advanced bookings; tickets are sold on the spot with cash payment and first come, first serve. The elephants can take two to three passengers at a time depending on your weight. You have to be at least two people at a time. If you come alone, you will be paired up with other tourists to balance the saddle.

Landmine Museum

Time: 30 minutes.
Importance: On show are a number of landmines and other ordinance that were used during the Vietnam and Khmer Rouge war.
My Impression: The landmine museum is small, but packs a lot of information on ordinances that were used in Cambodia. It is shocking to hear that there are still deaths from unexploded ordinance at the time of writing. (2015).
Open: 8 am to 5 pm.
Best time to visit: Anytime, but recommend combining it with a visit to Banteay Srei temple.
Entry Fee: $5.
GPS: 13°32'22.2"N 103°56'43.8"E.

The landmine museum is a small museum located 6.5 kilometers from Road 810 that goes to Banteay Samre and 21.2 kilometers from National Road 6.

Look for a small entrance at a parking area with large bombs that form an honor guard to the entrance (on your right when coming from town.)

The museum houses a number of explosives, shells, landmines, and other items that were used during the Vietnam War as well as when the Khmer Rouge was in power. In addition to a central area that holds anti-personnel landmines that are designed to maim as well as anti-tank landmines (descriptions are given on white boards). Anti-personnel mines were, at times, also used as booby traps and placed below an anti-tank mine. When deminers found an anti-tank mine and dug it out, the anti-personnel mine below would explode as the deminer lifted the anti-tank mine up. A good movie to get is *Bombhunters*, sold here if in stock or at ATC mall in town at the video shop on the second level. The museum has a small shop where you can buy souvenirs as well as a number of displays that show how deminers and soldiers look in full gear.

The entry fee is used to help clear landmines. The current cost is $30 million a year for demining. It is estimated that there are up to six million mines or unexploded ordinance left, and it will take up to 20 years to clear. Battambang, Pailin, and Banteay Meanchey are some of the worst affected areas. As the landmine museum is on the same road as Banteay Srei, Kbal Spean and Kulen waterfall, a visit to the museum can easily be done when seeing one of these places.

Miniature Golf

Time: 45 minutes to 2 hours.
Importance: Only miniature golf course and water slide in Siem Reap.
My Impression: The miniature golf course is a short distance out of town, and features a Khmer restaurant as well as a water slide and small swimming pool. The place is ideal for kids as the waterslide is a plastic one that is blown up with air, like a jumping castle.
Open: 8 am until 5 pm.
Fee: $5 for one round. $8 for two rounds. $10 for three rounds, per person. Kids are $4, $6, and $8 respectively.
Best time to visit: Early morning or late afternoon.
Tel: +855(0)12302330.
GPS: 13°20'41.8700" N 103°52'42.6600" E.

Angkor Wat Putt is a short distance out of town. The course is made interesting by having miniature models of some of the temples at a few of the holes.

The grounds have a small Khmer restaurant that also sells snacks as well as an aboveground swimming pool and a blowup water slide.

The place is ideal for a getaway from temples and markets, especially if you have kids or if your hotel does not have a swimming pool. The slide is $2 an hour. As the slide is directly opposite of the putt-putt course in the same grounds, you can let the kids have fun while you try to get a hole in one.

Although the course may not rival some that I have seen in larger cities, it is still fun and something to do for an hour or two.

For the professional club swingers, there is an excellent golf course a short distance out of town. See golf course under additional attractions.

Museum

Time: 45 minutes to 2 hours.
Importance: Main museum in Siem Reap. It holds a number of artifacts that span a great deal of the Khmer empire history from the first king.
My Impression: The museum pales in comparison to other museums I have visited, such as the one in New York. However, it does have a number of artifacts found in a number of temples in Cambodia, and is the best place to explore the history of Cambodia. Compared to its size, the entry fee is a bit steep; however, if you love history, it is worth it.
Open: 8 am to 5 pm.
Best time to visit: Anytime.
Entry Fee: $11.
GPS: 13°22'00.5"N 103°51'37.1"E.

The museum is situated 550 meters down Charles De Gualle Rd (the road that goes to Angkor Wat) from the roundabout where the road crosses National Road 6.

The museum houses a number of different artifacts and statues with information about the history of the Khmer Kings who built the temples. A room simulates the rising and setting sun over the Angkor Wat Temple by means of projectors and lights.

There is a small coffee shop on location as well as a souvenir shop. No photos are allowed inside, and cameras are to be left in a storage space provided. The museum is more for people interested in the history of Khmer Kings as well as Angkor Wat. A good movie to get is *Kingdom of Cambodia: History of Angkor Wat*, sold here when in stock or at ATC mall at the video store on the second level.

Although the museum has a number of artifacts to see, the main attraction is the rich information on Khmer history as well as the different building styles used over time.

New Market/Phsar Kandal

Time: 45 minutes to 2 hours.

Importance: Main tourist market for jewelry and souvenirs, as well as art.

My Impression: This market does not hide the fact that it is solely geared towards tourists. Prices are a bit higher than you would find in the old market; however, there is a larger verity of tourist goods. It is also one of the best places to get paintings from. There is a fresh fruit juice shop at the back, right next to a massage place. Have your tired feet massaged while you rejuvenate your body with a fresh fruit juice blend.

Open: 8 am to 5 pm. (Some shops stay open until 8 pm).

Best time to visit: Anytime, however, at night, the lights on the river and bridges are worth a visit in itself.

GPS: 13°21′9.3300″ N 103°51′18.8600″ E.

Across the river from the central market, is the New Market. This place is far more upscale and cleaner than the old market and mostly sells jewelry, clothing, backpacks, and paintings.

There are a few massage places and a shop selling fresh fruit juices. If you are looking for jewelry, this is the place to go. At the back near the fruit juice shop are a number of shops selling paintings. You can try to haggle over the price a bit, as most are inflated.

There is one ATM machine just outside the complex. Note that there are no fruit or meat shops here or shops selling pots and pans, as in the central market. In the middle of the market is a small restaurant that sells hamburgers, sandwiches, and coffee. The food is okay, although a bit overpriced for what you can find on Sok San Road or some of the places on Pub Street.

At night, the bridges over the river as well as lanterns in the water are lit up and make for a must-see attraction.

Night Market

Time: 45 minutes to 3 hours.
Importance: Main night market in town. Have a number of handmade items that are only sold at the night market, such as impressively embroidered purses and custom made flip-flops as well as sand bottles (bottles with multicolored sand in, to your asking).
My Impression: The market is clean, and the quality of the items sold good. I found a number of items here, such as hand-embroidered purses that I did not see anywhere else in Cambodia.
Open: 6 pm until 8 to 10 pm depending on the shops.
Best time to visit: 6:30 pm onwards.
GPS: 13°21'18.2700" N 103°51'14.9100" E.

Siem Reap really comes alive at night. A whole section opens up at night that is something to go and have a look at even if you are not intending to buy anything.

Do know that prices are even more jacked up, as most tourists are caught in the moment and may have had a beer or two already. Haggle with prices or buy at the central or old market in the day.

The night market starts at Sivatha Boulevard, near Sok San Road (Road 50) corner, and spans a few roads down. There are massive light signs hanging in the street showing you where to go.

The market (section to the left of the picture) has a number of stalls that sell handmade items you can only find in the night market, such as custom flip-flops on the spot where you pick your sole, strap, and clips yourself from a number of different options. There are also high-quality, handmade purses that are richly decorated with embroidering. Most nights, there are also artists who make bracelets and sand bottles on the spot for you.

There are a number of Khmer restaurants to choose from, and they cater to budget and upscale tastes. Normally, you will find massage places all over, and some are open until midnight.

Old Market at road 6/Phsar Leu

Time: 45 minutes to 2 hours.

Importance: Main market in Siem Reap if you want to get anything, especially if you are staying in Siem Reap a bit longer.

My Impression: The market is massive, and has everything you need for everyday living. What you cannot find here, you will find at the shops in road 6 near the market. Prices are lower here than the other two markets, however, it still pays to learn what Khmer numbers look like, as if you ask the price, it will most likely be given as double the actual price.

Open: 8 am until 5 pm.

Best time to visit: Anytime.

GPS: 13°21'40.3300" N 103°52'05.7000" E.

This market is a bit of a distance out on Route 6 and is worth it if you are staying in Siem Reap and want to save a few dollars.

If you have not seen a large market yet, then it will be an experience walking though the market and seeing wedding dresses and meat hanging on rails.

There is a money exchange place across the road at a smaller market that gives reasonable rates. Note that US dollars are accepted all over Cambodia.

This market is not geared towards tourists, so if you are looking for a souvenir to take home, you are better off looking at the central market or the night market. This market is, however, one of the best places to get cheap clothing and shoes.

Note that the hygiene of the meat sold here is even more suspect than the central market. Thus, get there early in the morning and buy from one of the stalls that are a bit cleaner.

To get here, follow National Road 6 out of town and look for the market on the right. (You will see a large area where motorcycles park and a row of fruit stands in the front.) Watch out, as people zoom through the market in the back where the meat section is with motorcycles.

Pottery

Time: 1 to 2 hours.
Importance: One of the best places to learn how to make a clay pot, or having fun in trying.
My Impression: The teachers are skilled and patient, allowing you to have loads of fun while trying to make your masterpiece.
Open: 8 am to 5 pm.
Best time to visit: Anytime, with booking.
Cost: From $20.
GPS: 13°22′4.1300″ N 103°51′39.6000″ E.

Khmer Ceramics is a good place to unwind and let your creative talents flow. The place offers different courses for beginners to more advanced potters. They have a shuttle that can pick you up and drop you off at your hotel as well as bring your masterpiece for you when done.

You can elect to make one or two pieces, which will then be baked for you and delivered to your hotel. What better souvenir to take home than a handmade, small pot that you made yourself in Cambodia?

If you are not one to get your hands dirty, there is a shop at the back where you can buy handmade clay pots and a number of other items for very reasonable prices. Note that prices are very low and set, so please do not argue about the prices.

Making your own clay pot, along with cooking classes and bicycle tours, are possibly some of the best things you can do in Siem Reap other than seeing temples.

If you do not want to make a clay pot, then you can buy handmade ceramic bead jewelry from
Clay Cult.
Website: http://www.claycult.com/
Tel: +855 17419904 or +855 95779369.
Open: Monday to Saturday from 9 to 12 am and 1 to 5 pm.

Pub Street and Pub Alley

Time: The time it takes to drink a beer, or two.

Importance: Pubs, restaurants, and souvenir shops all in one road, what more do you need?

My Impression: Even though the name Pub Street may sound like a place for young backpackers just seeking 50c draft beers, it is not really. The real backpacker hangouts are more in Sok San road a short distance away. Although Pub Street has a number of bars, there are a number of upscale restaurants (such as Temple) as well as a few souvenir shops.

Open: Early until late at night (depending on shops and bars).

Best time to visit: During the day for a quiet meal, and at night for the action.

GPS: 13°21'16.7200" N 103°51'17.1300" E.

Pub Street is just off Sivatha Boulevard and, like the night market, really comes alive at night.

The road is one of the most famous in town for both good cuisine and cheap draft beers. On most Friday and Saturday nights, you will find groups of young backpackers doing pub crawling from bar to bar.

The street, as its name says, is lined with eating and drinking places with a few shops to get a massage thrown in. If you are looking to meet fellow travelers, this is the place to be at night.

Getting to Pub Street is easy. It starts near the top of Sivatha Boulevard with huge lit signs pointing towards it all over town. Any tuk tuk driver will know where it is.

Although the street is reasonably well patrolled until around 10:00 pm, you are advised not to wander into side allies at night, especially if you are alone. If you are a bit tipsy, take a tuk tuk back to your hotel rather than a motor scooter taxi. Many tourists injure themselves badly each year from falling off the back scooters while drunk.

Tonle Sap Lake

Time: 3 to 4 hours, (including 25 min ride to the lake each way.)
Importance: Tonle Sap Lake is the largest fresh water lake in Cambodia, and in fact, South East Asia.
My Impression: Tourist trap, big time.
Open: Around 8 am to 5 pm.
Best time to visit: Wet season if you have to go.
Entry Fee: $30 and up, see text. Tuk tuk around $10.
GPS: 13°16′11.0100″ N 103°49′18.8900″ E for ticket office to Chong Khneas.

Tonle Sap Lake is the largest freshwater lake in Cambodia and, in fact, Southeast Asia. It is a source of income and food for millions of people. It is also an unusual lake, as it changes its flow twice a year as water enters and leaves the lake. Water levels can change by as much as 10 meters between dry and wet seasons, and the surface area is from 2,700 to 16,000 square kilometers. The lake has over 300 fish species and over 100 bird species.

The lake itself is not the main attraction. The main attraction is a number of floating villages along the banks. Although there are a number of villages to visit, if you mention Tonle Sap Lake or village to a tuk tuk driver or tour operator, you will most likely be taken to Chong Khneas. However, this is a tourist trap, and there are other options if you are interested. Following is a short description of Chong Khneas (the main village you will be taken to) as well as descriptions of a few other options.

Chong Khneas

As mentioned in the Tonle Sap section, there are a number of villages along the lake that can be visited, however, as Chong Khneas village is the most popular, I will cover it in detail, with some information on the other villages.

The lake boat ticket office is 12.8 Km from Siem Reap, on route 63. It is sad to say that this is a massive rip off scheme. The tourist police took over the boat operation in 2003, and prices have gone up dramatically. The price at current is $30 for the boat ride, although this bounces up and down at will. The boat operator and guide taking you out see nothing, so do not be surprised if they ask you for $20 each at the end of the trip.

The trip itself consists of a boat ride along the edge of the lake, to a floating restaurant, crocodile farm, and shop. The prices for goods here are not too bad. However, if you are unlucky, you will be taken to the floating goods shop close by, where you are asked to buy rice and food for the local kids. The floating goods shops ask $2 /kg for rice that sells for under $0.50c if you buy per kg, in the market and even less, if you buy bulk. Even if you are taken to the floating shop next to the floating school, you are still charged more than double ($1.1 /kg) for the rice than the going rate it goes for in the market.

You can take a canoe for a 15-minute tour in the mangroves for around $12. This money goes directly to the community, and not the tourist police. Overall, if you can only do this village, it is better than nothing, but do know it is overpriced, and rather buy rice at the market and donate it to one of the schools in town to maximize your donation dollar.

Be forewarned, that their tactics are very good, and if you are unsuspecting and soft hearted and new to Cambodia, you can easily wonder where $300 went after the trip, as was my case.

At the Floating market and restaurant, there is a small crocodile farm on-board, where crocodiles are kept for a number of years, before being served as a dish or a handbag. There is a top deck, where you can sit and have a nice view of the lake and the surrounding area.

Prek Toal/Bird Sanctuary

Prek Toal is the village closest to the bird sanctuary, and is located about an hour west of Chong Khneas. Tours are run to the sanctuary, with overnight stay possible, however this is expensive. Prices are around $35 out to the village, with between $60 and $165 for a trip to the bird sanctuary. The sanctuary has been called the single most important breeding ground in Southeast Asia for globally threatened large water birds. The best time to go is in the dry season. See *Tara River Boat.*
Website: http://www.taraboat.com/prek-toal/

Kompong Phluk

Kompong Phluk is about 25 kilometers east of Chong Khneas, and is a permanent village as to a floating village. The village is almost exclusively reached by boat for most of the year, and due to being further along, less visited than Chong Kneas. Prices are around $30 to $40 for a good tour package. Tara River Boat as mentioned before do trips out to the village.

Note, that as Prek Toal, you can get a boat from Chong Khneas without a tour operator, but this boat is operated by the tourist police, and will cost you normally the same or more than a tour operator, with no tour guide for the price. Note that some operators avoid the Chong Khneas boat launch, and use the Roluos village entry. However, during the dry months from December to July, you will need to take a miserable rough ride on a motorbike over the dry lakebed where the lake receded. Rather go to Kompong Khleang in the dry months if not leaving from Ching Khneas.

Kompong Khleang

Kompong Khleang is next to Tonle Sap town, and east of Kompong Phluk. It is the largest permanent settlement on the lake, and accessible by water and by land most of the year. The best time is in the dry season, when hundreds of buildings stand several meters above the water. As it is further out than Kompong Phluk, prices are around $40 to $50 for a good tour. Since it is the largest village on the lake, it gives the best perspective of living on a lake, and due to its distance, is one of the least visited villages. As with the other villages, many tour operators run tours to the villages.

Moat Klais

Moat Klais is the last village in Siem Reap province, on the southeastern end of the lake, and several hours by boat from Siem Reap. The village is only accessible by boat, and is a floating Vietnamese village. Being remote, tours are in the $130 and up, with a pick-up normally from Kompong Khleang or Kompong Phluk. There are, however, many mangrove canals and a small lake itself to see, and a good place for bird lovers that want to get away from other tourists.

Kbal Taol

Kbal Taol is a floating village at the southern end of Battambang province, near the southern end of the bird sanctuary. The best time to visit is during the wet season, when the village moves inland, and becomes surrounded by thick foliage and crisp clear water. Trips to the village are expensive, with an overnight trip running around $200 per person or $300 for two. As almost no tourists come here, it is mostly unspoiled wetlands with very friendly villagers.

Pursat

Pursat province is on the other side of the lake, and has a number of floating villages in the province. If you are in Pursat, then many of the villages can be seen for cheaply as almost no tourists come here, and the place is not controlled, at the moment, by the government or tourist police. Peach Kantil, Kbal Taol and Prek Kra are good ones to see, but only accessible by boat and expensive compared to ones accessible by motorbike for around $10, such as Kompong Luong.

War Museum

Time: 30 minutes.
Importance: The museum shows a number of ordinances used during the Khmer Rouge occupation.

My Impression: A small museum that have a number of stripped down tanks and artillery piece, however, still worth a visit.
Open: 8 am to 5 pm.
Best time to visit: Anytime.
Entry Fee: $5.
Website: http://www.warmuseumcambodia.com/
GPS: 13°22'49.0"N 103°49'43.2"E for turn from N6.
GPS: 13°23'16.0"N 103°49'59.1"E For last turn.

The war museum is 5.14 kilometers from the town center and has a number of tanks, armored personnel carriers, small arms, a helicopter, a fighter jet, and some anti-aircraft guns on display. Guides are free when available. A tuk tuk should cost around $5, but a trip to here can be included with a trip to Angkor Wat.

Head 3.6 kilometers on National Road 6 towards the airport from the crossing between N6 and Sivatha Road. Turn right at Royal Angkor Resort onto a side road and then head 1 kilometer down the dirt road until you see a sign for the museum on the left.

The first display that you will come to has a number of landmines and other explosive ordinances used during the war. From there, you will pass a few artillery pieces as well as an empty shell of an old mobile missile launcher. The anti-aircraft guns are still in good order. You will find a shell of a Mil Mi-8 helicopter in the back left corner as well as a shell of a MiG-19 fighter jet.

As something else than temples to see, it is worth the visit if you have the time to spare.

West Baray/Baray Toek Thla

Time: 15 minutes.

Importance: Is the largest fabricated body of water at Angkor.

My Impression: Having lived in Cambodia for more than a year, it is impressive to see the difference between wet and dry season. The spot is a frequent hangout for my friends, and me, and a ride on the lake is worth it.

Open: Boats run from around 7 am to 5 pm.

Best time to visit: Anytime, but the wet season is the most spectacular.

Date: Beginning to middle of the 11th century.

King: Suryavarman I.

GPS: 13°25'29.1"N 103°47'05.9"E for boat dock.

West Baray is 17.6 square kilometers and is the largest fabricated body of water at Angkor. It has an average depth of 7 meters and holds around 123 million cubic liters of water.

Even today, the baray is a major source of fish for the locals as well as a spot to swim, picnic, and relax. The baray water level drops by meters between the dry and wet seasons.

The boat dock to catch a boat out to West Mebon is situated here. From Siem Reap, head 8.3 kilometers along National Road 6 towards the airport and then take a right into a side road just before a small bridge at the turn-off listed (towards the Paradise Eco Resort). Travel an additional 3 kilometers along the road until you come to the baray wall. The dock is opposite the water channel that feeds water from the baray to Siem Reap City. There are a few Khmer restaurants to eat at on the top as well as a number of shops to buy clothing. However, one of the main attractions here is the hammocks that are situated at water level, where you can relax or go for a swim.

The baray in the dry season. February 2014.

As can be seen from the first picture, the water level is all the way up to the trees and Khmer restaurants on the left-hand side in the wet season. The picture above was taken below the water line from the cement walkway, as seen in the first picture.

Additional attractions

As always, taste differs, and what one-person finds as must do, may not be to the liking of another person. In addition, there is always something else to do. Following are a number of additional things you can do in Siem Reap if you have the time.

Cooking Classes

For those that want to learn a new dish, or see how local dishes are made, a cooking class is the perfect way to spend a few hours. There are a number of tours offered around town, some allowing you to visit a local village, where you may prepare and eat lunch with locals, while others offers cooking classes in a kitchen of a local hotel.

One of the tours to look into is from Sense & Spice. **http://www.beyonduniqueescapes.com/.** They offer Am, Pm, or full day classes. Prices are from $24 for half a day to $40 for a full day, with evening classes upon request. +855(0) 77562565 or +855(0) 63969269. **booking@beyonduniqeescapes.com**

Kick Boxing

Few visitors to Cambodia know that Thai kickboxing (including many Thai dishes) originated in Cambodia. If you want to see some action, then head to CTN Angkor Arena. Tickets are $15 a person, and matches are normally fought on weekends and at night. +855(0) 12 601969, +855(0) 78 555303, +855(0) 78 555301. GPS: 13.372612 103.861770.

Concert

If you are in town on a Saturday night and want to see a local concert, then head to Kantha Bopha Academy. It starts every Saturday from 7:15 pm. GPS: 13.375353 103.861787

Golf Course

For those that love two swing a club, head to Angkor Golf Resort. They have a nice restaurant where you can have breakfast and lunch. There are a 18 and a 9 hole course. Prices are $125 and $88 respectively for walk-in green fee. A caddy is $8 to $12, with club rental $15 to $25 and cart rental at $18 to $36 (9 or 18 holes depending).
Website: www.angkor-gold.com.
Tel: +855(0)63 767688 or +855(0)63 767689.

Email: info@angkor-golf.com.
GPS: 13.367708 103.816650.

Helicopter Rides

Two main helicopter operators do tours all around Cambodia, with a few smaller ones doing day tours. The two operators listed below, do scheduled flights from $90, for an 8-minute flight that only does Angkor Wat temple, to $485, for a 48-minute flight that covers Angkor Wat and nearby temples such as Banteay Srei, Phnom Kulen, Roluos Group, Tonle Sap floating village, and Phnom Krom.

Both operators offer pick-ups at your hotel, and depart from an airstrip near the Siem Reap international airport. Both operators also offer remote temple flights, to temples such as Banteay Chhmar and Preah Vihear. You can also rent the helicopters for filming, corporate events, survey flights, and medivac emergencies.

A flight over Angkor Wat will give you a unique perspective of how vast the complex really is.

Note, all flights must be pre-booked.

Helicopters Cambodia
Website: http://www.helicopterscambodia.com/html/
+855 (0)12 814 500
+855 (0)23 213 706

Helistar Cambodia
Website: http://helistarcambodia.com/
+855 (63) 966 072
+855 (23) 431 011

Flight of the Gibbon

Time: 3 to 4 hours.
Price: $109.
Website: http://www.flightofthegibbon.com/
GPS: 13°27'11.4"N 103°52'59.4"E.

Flight of the Gibbon, is a jungle orientation, by cables and ropes. You are strapped into a harness, and then taken through the forest, while being suspended in the air. You will go from base to base, with the longest distance between bases 300m. An experienced guide accompanies you at all times, who gives you information about the animals and trees found in the forest. The experience itself takes around three hours, with orientation and gear kit up an additional ½ hour. If you have the time and the money, it is something different from temple seeing, and is a safe way to see the jungle, without trekking through it.

 Flight of the Gibbon is directly past the small side road for Ta Nei temple.

Horse Riding
Time: 2 to 15 minutes in Angkor Wat, or longer if going with an operator in the countryside.
Price: About $1 for a picture only. $5 for a ride around Angkor Temple.
GPS: 13°24'46.3"N 103°51'50.5"E.

Inside the grounds of Angkor Wat Temple, you can ride a horse, or just sit on it and have your picture taken. The service moves around, but is normally just before the temple, near either of the two libraries that are situated at either side of the causeway that leads to the temple. The horse riding and picture opportunity are a big hit with many kids. Note, there is normally only one, to two horses, thus it is not a service where you can rent a horse and go exploring on your own. The owner, to avoid it running away with you or your kids, also walks the horse.

As this is a popular service, there is no pre-booking, and it is first come first serve. If the owner is not to be found, he may be with other customers walking around Angkor Temple, wait a while, or come back at another time.

If you want to ride a horse in the countryside, then see
Happy Ranch Horse Farm.
Website: http://www.thehappyranch.com/.
Email: info@thehappyranhc.com.
Tel: +855(0)12 920002 or +855(0)16 920002 or +855(0)97 7920002.
They give rides from $28 for one-hour rides, to $69 rides for four hours.

Yoga and Reiki

If Yoga and Reiki interests you, then you are in luck. There are a number of retreats where you can stay and get away from city life. Resident Reiki and Yoga instructors offer courses at the retreats on most nights, and will take your meditation to a new level.

One of the places to look at is
Angkor Bodhi Tree Retreat.
Website: http://www.angkorbodhitree.com/
Email: Angkor.bodhitree@gmail.com
Tel: +855(0)88 6065906.

Body massage

Lastly, but definitely something you have to do, is get a massage. There are a number of massage places around Siem Reap. Most offer air-conditioned places, with prices starting at $1 for 15 minutes. This normally includes a hand and foot massage. For a full-body massage, a one-hour session is normally needed. Some of the more upmarket hotels have spas that offer their own massages; however, they are normally pricier. Note, Cambodia is not Thailand, and $10 love you long time is illegal. If this is what you want, then spend $6 on a bus to Bangkok and go to cowboy town.

About the Author

Anton Swanepoel @ Pol Pot's house on the mountains in Thailand, and on his way to Preah Vihear Temple.

An ex software developer that left the corporate world, Anton for seven years worked as a technical diving instructor in the Cayman Islands. He is a Tri-Mix instructor for multiple agencies, and has dived to over 400ft on open circuit. While on Grand Cayman, he started his passion, writing, and currently has 20 books published.

In Jan 2014, Anton moved to Siem Reap, Cambodia, to go for his dream of being a full-time writer. Currently living cheaply off his savings, he loves to laugh, travel, and often worries too much.

Follow his adventures and share some laughs, tears, and moments of a lifetime. *www.antonswanepoelbooks.com/blog.*

More Books by Anton

www.antonswanepoelbooks.com

Novels
Laura and The Jaguar Prophecy (Book 1)
Laura and The God Code (Book 2)
Laura and the Spear of Destiny (Book 3)

Peru Travel
Machu Picchu: The Ultimate Guide to Machu Picchu

Travel Tips
Angkor Wat & Cambodia

Motorbike Travel
Motorcycle: A Guide Book To Long Distance And Adventure Riding
Motorbiking Cambodia & Vietnam

Cambodia Travel
Angkor Wat: 20 Must Ssee Temples
Angkor Wat Temples
Angkor Wat Archaeological Park
Angkor Wat & Cambodia Temples
Kampot, Kep and Sihanoukville
Kampot: 20 Must See Attractions
Battambang: 20 Must See Attractions
Phnom Penh: 20 Must See Attractions
Siem Reap: 20 Must See Attarctions
Dangerous Loads
Sihanoukville 20 must see attraions
Kep 10 Must See Attractions

Vietnam Travel
Vietnam Caves
Ha Long Bay
The Perfumed Pagoda
Phong Nha Caves

Thailand
Bangkok: 20 Must See Attractions
Ayutthaya: 20 Must See Attractions
The Great Buddha

Laos
Vientiane: 20 Must See Attractions

Diving Books
Dive Computers
Gas Blender Program
Deep and Safety Stops, and Gradient Factors
Diving Below 130 Feet
The Art of Gas Blending

Writing Books
Supercharge Your Book Description (Grab Attention and Enhance Sales)

Self Help Books
Ear Pain
Sea and Motion Sickness

Printed in Great Britain
by Amazon.co.uk, Ltd.,
Marston Gate.